Pygmy Leaf Chameleon as Pets

Caring For Your Pygmy Leaf Chameleons

Pygmy Leaf facts, care, breeding, nutritional information, tips, and more!

By Lolly Brown

Foreword

Pygmy Leaf Chameleons are one of the smallest pet reptiles you can possibly keep at home. The Pygmy leaf chameleons' cute size, its inexpensive purchase price, and its maintenance are some of the major factors on why it is attractive to potential chameleon or reptile owners in general.

However, keeping chameleons as pets may be viewed as unconventional, and due to the lack of common knowledge about these creatures, some people tend to think that keeping one might be rather difficult. Indeed, for first time owners they could be hard to manage. In this book you'll be easily guided on understanding your Pygmy leaf chameleons; their behaviors, their characteristics, how you should feed and care for them and a whole lot more.

Embark on a wonderful journey of sharing your life with Pygmy Leaf Chameleons. Learn to maximize the great privilege of living with one and be able to share this unique and unforgettable experience just like many chameleon pet owners that came before you!

Table of Contents

Introduction

Pygmy Leaf chameleons are micro - creatures that one may hardly notice – it's a chameleon after all. What more if you walk out in the world, or go into your friend's room and you saw it? It may never come across as a pet. In fact, you might try to keep it away like some kind of an insect that graced your shoulder. The only common knowledge about chameleons in general is that they are those reptile creatures that have the ability to blend in with its environment. It's a cool feature but in reality it's a defense mechanism for these animals when they are in trouble. Since there is a lack of extensive knowledge about these animals; let alone managing or keeping one as a house pet, people usually think that it is rather hard to manage.

The number of captive breed were very low back then, and female chameleons are somewhat known as quite delicate to handle. The mere fact that none of your friends, or neighbors own one is already can pose as a challenge because you may need to research on your own, and you have no one to turn to that is nearby your area – thanks to the internet, you can now connect with fellow chameleon owners or reptile experts through various forums and social media. However, even if resources are available, you as a first time reptile owner might still find it difficult to take care of a small and quite "invisible" pet, which is why this book is perfect for you!

The Pygmy Leaf Chameleons are more than just an invisible pet; it is docile, can be friendly and probably a much more interesting companion than the usual pets. They are easy to maintain in terms of costs, and housing, and hey you'd be surprise because they can be very great family pets as well!

Before you bring a Pygmy Leaf chameleon home, however, you should be a responsible pet reptile owner and learn everything you can about this breed and how to care for it properly. Fortunately, this ultimate guide will teach you on how to be the best Pygmy Leaf chameleon owner you can be!

Inside this book, you will find tons of helpful information about different types of Pygmy Leaf chameleons; how they live, how to deal with them and realize the great benefits of owning one!

This book includes information about creating the ideal enclosures and proper feeding for your chameleons as well as tips for breeding and taking care of them. You will also find in-depth health information for the breed including common health problems affecting it and the treatment options available.

The amazing world of Pygmy Leaf Chameleon awaits! Get your camouflage on – your eyesight will be tested!

Glossary of Chameleon Terms

0.0.0 - represents male.female.unsexed. For example, 2.1 Furcifer pardalis means 2 male and 1 female panther chameleons.

Acrodont - having teeth that are anchored to the mandible (jaw bone) without individual sockets. Unique to certain orders of reptiles, including chameleons.

Advanced Species - these species are best left to keepers with a number of years of experience with intermediate level chams as they have unique husbandry requirements and limited numbers in captivity and possibly in the wild as well. They are very difficult to keep and even more so to breed. Examples: montium, quadricornis, mellers, etc.

Ambient Temperature - the average temperature of the room or area around the chameleon that is unaffected by the basking light.

Arboreal - means "living in trees". The majority of chameleon species fall into this category. These are species that spend most of their time in the middle to higher levels of the forest and rarely go to the ground aside from egg laying. They hunt, drink and mate in the branches of trees.

Captive caging for arboreal animals should be taller than wide and include many branches to accommodate this lifestyle.

Aspirate - refers to inhaling liquid or food into the trachea, which can lead to choking, pneumonia, or death.

Bask - the full body absorption of heat from the sun, or overhead light source, by reptiles. It helps to regulate body temperature which in turn promotes proper digestion and a healthy metabolism.

Captive Bred (CB) - these animals have been bred, born and raised in captivity. They tend to be healthier and more hardy compared to WC/LTC specimens, as they are used to captive conditions and do not have heavy parasite burdens. Captive bred animals have also avoided the heavy stresses related to capture and exportation.

Captive Hatched (CH) - these are offspring from eggs hatched in captivity but were laid by a wild caught female who was gravid when imported. This also applies to babies born in captivity to a wild caught female.

Casque - French for 'helmet', the top of the head of all chameleons is referred to as a casque.

Clutch - one group of eggs or the siblings that hatched from that one group.

Deworming - medical treatment of intestinal parasites diagnosed by a fecal exam.

Diapause - simulating a winter season by lowering temperatures for incubating eggs in the middle segment of incubation. It is required by some species.

Dripper - a vessel that allows water to drip down into the cage for the chameleon to drink. May be as simple a hole in the bottom of a cup, or commercially produced product like the "Little Dripper".

Dusting - applying a powdered vitamin or mineral supplement to feeder insects immediately before feeding them to a chameleon.

Dysecdysis - a problem with shedding that result in retained skin that should have fallen off and may cause additional problems such as appendage stricture. Usually results from improper temperature and humidity parameters.

Ectotherm - an animal that controls body temperature through external means since it cannot generate its own body heat (cold-blooded).

Edema - an accumulation of fluid under the skin, usually in the gular region, suspected to be caused by vitamin imbalance or organ failure.

Eggbound - a serious condition for female egg laying chameleons where for medical, nutritional or environmental reasons they are unable to lay their eggs. Fatal if not treated.

Expert Species - these are species left only for the most experienced keepers, as they are challenging in all aspects. These chameleons are also highly limited in their captive population due to their care needs and may be endangered or threatened in their natural habitat. They are nearly impossible to breed. Ex: Parsons

Farm Raised (FR) - this term can imply different things depending on the source, and resellers may label these animals CB or WC, depending on the personal opinion of the reseller and what is more profitable. These animals typically need the medical care of WCs, but tend to be somewhat better adapted to captive conditions than WC animals.

Fecal - generally refers to diagnostic testing of a fresh fecal (poop) sample for the presence of microscopic eggs of intestinal parasites performed by a vet.

Gout - a medical condition often recognized by swollen, painful joints caused by crystallization of uric acid crystals within the joints. This has been associated with excessive dietary protein, chronic dehydration, imbalance of calcium, phosphorus, vitamin A, vitamin D and/or kidney disease. This is a very painful disease and there is not an effective treatment.

Gravid - carrying eggs, or pregnant in the case of live-bearing species.

Gular - the region under the neck just in front of the arms.

Gutloading - providing a healthy balanced diet high in calcium to feeder insects before feeding them to the chameleon so that the nutrients are passed to the chameleon.

Hemipenes - paired reproductive organ of male lizards in the order Squamata, like chameleons.

Husbandry - the practice of creating a proper captive

environment and maintaining appropriate humidity, temperature, lighting, good nutrition, etc.

Impaction - intestines are clogged (impacted) with a non-digestible material, such as dirt, bark, rocks, excessive chitin, etc that prevents the digestion and passage of food. May be life-threatening if not treated.

Intermediate Species - these species are for more experienced keepers, having some unique husbandry requirements challenging enough that experience in general care of chameleons is recommended before attempting.

Lethargy - decrease in activity or sleeping more than usual, often associated with signs of illness.

Litter - the group of siblings from an viviparous species.

Locale - a natural geographic location that represents specific color variation within the same species, usually the result of geographic isolation. Panther chameleons are commonly labeled by locale. The panther locales are named after geographic areas in Madagascar and each represents a unique color pattern. For example: Nosy Be chameleons are generally very blue and come from an island off Madagascar called Nosy Be.

Long Term Captive (LTC) - these are animals that have been in captivity over 8-12 months but were originally wild caught. They have usually adapted to captivity at this point, and are more stable at this stage than when originally imported since common health issues have been resolved.

MBD (metabolic bone disease) - condition of weak bones that break easily and overall metabolic illness due to lack of dietary calcium, imbalanced nutrition and/or lack of UVB rays. Serious problem leaving to permanent damage and death if not addressed quickly.

Montane - chameleon species existing in a more mountainous environment at higher altitudes, lower temperatures and higher relative humidity than traditional tropical species.

Morph - refers to the color pattern variations of chameleons within one species established by selective breeding in captivity for a particular trait. For example: translucent veiled chameleons.

Mouthrot (stomatitis) - an infection of the mouth that could be deep into the underlying bone and can spread to the rest of the body. Requires veterinary attention and antibiotics specific to the bacteria causing the infection.

Novice Species - chameleons in general are not beginner animals but those designated "novice" are considered the best "beginner" species in the hobby with large, stable captive populations relative to other species. They are relatively easy to breed as well. Examples: panther and veiled chameleons

Oviparous - mode of reproduction where embryos develop inside eggs that have been laid by the mother. Little to no development occurs inside the mother's body (ie., birds and most chameleon species).

Ovoviviparous - this mode of reproduction is not found in chameleons. Please see the definition for Viviparous.

Parietal Eye - a photoreceptive (able to sense light) scale on the top of the head that can sense light when the eyes are closed and may play a part in regulating circadian rhythm and hormone production for thermoregulation.

Prolapse - internal organ that has inverted on itself and protruded out of the body through the vent. A medical emergency that should be addressed asap.

Receptive - referring to a female being willing to breed with a male, often indicated by a distinct change in coloration depending on the species.

Rostral process - the crest of scales at the tip of the nose.

Shed (ecdysis) - the periodic shedding of the outer layer of skin in reptiles to allow for growth. Becomes less frequent as the reptile gets older.

Supplements - concentrated calcium or vitamins, usually in powdered form, to add value to the diet.

Tarsal Spur - a bump on the back of the hind feet of Veiled, Graceful, and some species of Flapneck chameleons. Only present on males.

Terrestrial - these are species that in the wild reside on the ground or in the lowest levels of the forest, like shrubbery, with some time spent on the ground. In captivity these species may take advantage of available height, but floorspace should be considered when designing housing. Very few chameleons fall into this category - mostly pygmy species.

Turret - the mobile portion of the eyeball covered in skin around the visible eye opening.

Urates - the white portion of the feces that is essentially concentrated urine. Yellow or orange color indicates dehydration.

Upper Respiratory Infection (URI) - an infection of the nasal cavity, trachea, and/or bronchi that manifests as lethargy, wheezing or popping noises while breathing and excess saliva in the mouth.

UVB - invisible ultraviolet rays emitted by the sun with a spectrum between 280-315nm, responsible for vitamin D synthesis in the skin to regulate calcium homeostasis. Critical to chameleon health.

Vent - common opening for the digestive, urinary and reproductive tract in birds and reptiles just under the base of the tail.

Vivarium - Latin for "place of life", a cage attempting to recreate the natural environment of the animal's native habitat.

Viviparous - mode of reproduction where embryos develop inside the mother's body until they are ready to be born, at which point the mother gives birth to live young that immediately break free of a membrane (ie., Jackson's chameleons).

Wild Caught (WC) - these are animals collected in the wild and exported from their native country - usually young adults. They will probably need to be treated for parasites and other medical conditions like dehydration, are very stressed, and may come in in very bad condition. They are best left for keepers with more experience, even if the species is considered Novice, for these reasons.

Zygodactyl feet - The arrangement of toes on the hands and feet where the 2nd and 4th digits point forward while the 1st and 3rd digits point backward. It is a misnomer that chameleons are zygodactyl. They actually have 5 digits fused into two groups on each foot. Their toe arrangement also alternates between front and hind limbs.

Chapter One: Getting to Know Pygmy Leaf Chameleons

Pygmy Leaf Chameleons may often times look like a frog, your outcast classmate, the new kid in school, your weird–at – first – but – turns – out – a – cool roommate, or unexpected sidekick. In whatever attitude or mood it appeals, you can expect it to be docile and it will definitely pique your interest. After all only interesting people will acquire an interesting kind of pet!

Pygmy leaf chameleons are may be relatively small and handy but it may not be the right choice for everyone.

Before you decide whether or not it might be the right

pet for you and your family, you need to learn and invest a significant amount of time in getting to know these creatures because it may not be suitable for first time chameleon owners; this breed has additional husbandry requirements which may be difficult if you haven't had any experience of handling a chameleon before.

In this chapter you will receive an introduction to the Pygmy leaf chameleons breed including some basic facts, different types info, as well as the brief history of how it came about. This information, in combination with the practical information about keeping chameleons in the next chapter, will help you decide if this is the perfect pet companion for you.

Facts about Pygmy Leaf Chameleons

In this section you'll find some interesting fun facts about Pygmy leaf chameleons, their breed origin, body features, breed types and history.

Pygmy leaf chameleons are also referred to as stump-tail chameleons. They are included in one of the smallest vertebrates known to mankind, and because of its relatively small size, keeping one as a pet is becoming more popular among reptile owners or reptile enthusiasts. It's not dangerous to handle if you're a first time reptile owner compared to a snake, and does not need too much maintenance compared to baby alligators or other quite large creatures. It's just handy, interesting, and can also be adorable. Chameleons are part of the iguana, and lizard family.

These creatures are native to montane forests, and often occupy lower shrubs, forest canopies or pretty much an area where there is little sunlight. You might think they are boring or not outspoken as an animal, but they stay out of everyone's way especially in the forests for a very good reason – they need to survive. Their small size can easily be eaten by all the wild creatures in the forests, or they can be simply stump to death by the huge creatures or things surrounding them.

Chameleons are generally known to disguise as ordinary things, making them quite "invisible" to the untrained eye. This evolution is for survival purposes; pygmy leaf chameleons for instance, have evolved to blend in and appear as a dead leaf, twigs or grasses found in their natural habitats so that they can't become an easy prey to the predators. This is also precisely the reason why the word and act of "camouflage" came about. The term is usually used in military to help them during combat – their camouflage uniform resembles that of a green plant, or terrain looking design for the mere purpose of not being seen by the enemy.

Humans found it fascinating that chameleons can hide in plain sight - a very interesting feature indeed, however if you are keeping one as a family pet, this can be quite challenging, so don't make them feel that they are threatened. Once you get to know them and their behaviors, they will eventually show you their true colors.

Fortunately, unlike other reptile creatures, most pygmy leaf chameleons are very docile and friendly animals. However, it is important to take note that since they are small and has "hiding" abilities; it should mostly be a pet for observation, much like a snake or a fish, and should not be handled unless necessary. Chameleons have a tendency to vibrate or buzz if they feel threatened by predators, insects or even by unnecessary human touch. They are quite sensitive, and what they lack in size makes up for their "superb abilities." The weird thing is if you are the owner or keeper, these creatures seem to be calm and doesn't feel intimidated, that's why it's important to get to know them so they can trust you.

Pygmy leaf chameleons being a reptile will have an unusual feeding habit or quite weird diet choices. For most people especially those who already have an experience in taking care reptiles like iguanas or lizards, Pygmy leaf chameleons are low maintenance and can be manageable that is why they are increasingly becoming popular as a pet despite its rarity. Like any other animals or family pets for that matter, pygmy leaf chameleons will need to be maintained and provided with adequate living environment, later on in this book we will tackle about the things you need in order to take care of your chameleon.

The pygmy leaf chameleon has a small and relatively elongated body type. Its adult length is about 8 – 9 cm or 3 – 3.5 inches. The smallest recorded pygmy chameleon so far is only 2.5 cm or 1 inch! These kinds of chameleons have a variety of shade that usually have a brown – color pattern and green skin surface to help them blend in their environment. They are called pygmy leaf because aside from their natural shade, they also resemble a leaf litter found in the forest floor.

Unfortunately, you can keep a pygmy leaf chameleon in just a few years. It's so short; you might think that knowing them doesn't even scratch the surface. Their average lifespan is between 1 and 3 years only. So if you do decide to acquire one or more and keep them as pets, don't get too attached because it will only break your heart, you're lucky if they lived up to their maximum.

One of the main factors that will keep your chameleon alive for at least a longer period is if you take care of it properly. Providing adequate shelter or living environment, proper diet, and care for when they are ill can definitely count if you want them to be around longer than the average. The breed is quite healthy in general as long as you take care of them properly. Like many pets, however, pygmy leaf chameleons are prone to health issues such as lethargy, Metabolic Bone Disease, skin problems, burns head and neck issues, and other body syndromes which will also be tackled in the next few chapters later on in this book.

Different Breeds of Pygmy Chameleons

In this section, you will learn the different breeds of Pygmy Chameleons – their physical characteristics, a snapshot of their origin and other important details you need to consider before acquiring them. Not all of the breeds listed below are suitable for you and some may also not be available in your area, so be sure to read the common facts and also try doing a bit of research if you have selected a pet pygmy breed. Chameleons are still rare at the time of this writing, you'd be lucky if you can find a variety of these breed in your location.

Bearded Pygmy Chameleonthese

Scientific Name: Rieppeleon brevicaudatus

Description:

- The bearded pygmy has a small "beard" of scales that protrude from the bottom of the chin in both sexes
- Generally light brown in color
- Has a striped or splotched pattern resembling a wilted leaf
- During courtship, tends to have shades of yellow, red and green

Range: Can be found in the Eastern Usambara and Uluguru Mountains of Tanzania.

Spectral Pygmy Chameleon

Scientific Name: Rhampholeon spectrum

Description:

- Spectral Pygmy Chameleon shades and patterns are usually browns, grey, and sometimes red tones.
- Diagonal stripes can be seen along their flanks

- A small, soft nasal process is present that appears like that of a small horn.
- Their tails are also longer than that of brevicaudatus.

Range: These breed can be found in Cameroon and Congo in wild forests.

Usambara Pitted Pygmy Chameleon

Scientific Name: Rhampholeon temporalis

Description:

- Rhampholeon temporalis are light brown or greyish in color.
- It has small diagonal stripes on the side of their bodies, and has broad and flat lips that look like a duck's beak.
- Their tails are also longer than that of brevicaudatus.

Range: This breed is only abundant in the humid Eastern Usambara Mountains.

History of Chameleons

During the 1990's chameleons in general are very hard to keep; they are famously known for being one of the shortest-lived pets and are doing poorly in captivity. It was impossible prior to the 90's to keep these animals alive, that's why they aren't popular as house pets back then. Nobody has any extensive knowledge on how to take care of these creatures – only scientists, vets or a wild life expert can probably take care of it, and breed them properly.

Fortunately today, because of modernization in technology and the internet, people eventually became interested in keeping these gentle creatures as pets. Several books and resources have become widely available for those who wanted to own one. Advanced keepers have dedicated in providing how – to guides about caring for a chameleon. The knowledge about these pets in the last two decades has blossomed and continues to expand thanks to the internet.

Today, the captive breed chameleons have a stable population with a variety of different species, it is still quite endangered, and some species are close to being extinct but overall pet owners can expect a relatively long term success in keeping one alive with the help of proper care and husbandry resources.

Quick Facts

Pedigree: evolved from an iguana and lizard species

Breed Size: relatively small and has a relatively elongated body structure similar to an iguana or a lizard

Length: adult length: 8 – 9 cm or 3 – 3.5 inches; smallest possible size: 2.5 cm or 1 inch

Weight: very light

Coat Length: coat is always changing depending on its environment; has a camouflage effect

Coat Texture: quite rough, scaly

Color: It has various shades of green, brown, yellow, grey and tone red.

Patterns/Markings: It has various patterns resembling its natural habitat; spots

Feet Type: similar to a lizard; small and webbed

Temperament: docile, gentle, friendly, sensitive, delicate

Strangers: may be threatened around strangers; may tend to vibrate or buzz

Other Pets: can get along with other chameleon breed with no more than one male in an enclosure. Not advisable to introduce to other house pets.

Training: cannot be trained, but behavior can be predicted

Exercise Needs: doesn't need exercise; recommended as an observation pet only

Health Conditions: generally healthy but predisposed to common illnesses such as lethargy, Metabolic Bone Disease, skin problems, burns head and neck issues, and other body syndromes

Lifespan: average 1 to 3 years

Chapter Two: Pygmy Leaf Chameleon Requirements

Interested in owning a Pygmy Leaf Chameleon? Fantastic! However, it is imperative that you see the maintenance costs before acquiring it as a pet as well as the laws involved before actually deciding to buy one.

In this chapter, you will get a whole lot of information on its pros and cons, its average associated costs as well as the laws you need to be aware of so that you will be well on your way to becoming a legitimate pygmy leaf chameleon pet owner. Ready? Read on!

Legal Requirements

If you are planning to acquire a pygmy leaf chameleon as your pet, there are certain restrictions and regulations that you need to be aware of. Legal requirements for keeping chameleon species may vary in different countries, regions, and states. It's highly recommended that you consult first with legal authorities near your area if you can or do a research online or locally.

In this section, we will provide you with an overview of the laws concerning chameleons in general.

CITES Laws for Chameleons

The Convention on International Trade in Endangered Species (CITES) for wild fauna and flora are the governing body that is responsible in taking care of all animal species especially the endangered ones. Almost all countries in major continents all over the world are a member of CITES including USA, Europe, Latin America, Asia and Australia. It is highly recommended that you have legal or proper documents regarding any animal or species you keep as pets to save you in case of any trouble.

CITES has 3 appendices, and each appendix contains a list of different species in different categories, and therefore has different rules when it comes to keeping, exporting and trading.

Chameleons such as the Pygmy Leaf fall under the CITES II appendix. CITES II includes species that can be traded freely but cannot be taken from the wild. Aside from the Pygmy Leaf other popular chameleon species kept as pets including Jackson's chameleon, Panther, and Veiled chameleons can be freely traded, and kept as long as they have the right documents or paper work.

The paperwork doesn't require any approval from wildlife authorities or organizations; you just need to simply provide a document stating the name, identity of the species or your chameleon as well as the name address, contact details and signature of the previous owner or where you bought it from. You need to also provide your own personal details and signature. This document needs to be kept for future reference by you the new owner until the chameleon is sold or if it dies.

Conservation Concerns and Legal Documents

Since chameleons in general are still very rare to find, very hard to breed and are quite delicate – not to mention that some of it are quite endangered already, conserving these species are a major topic and concern among wildlife enthusiasts. Chameleon breeders and pet owners believe that it is an owner's responsibility to take care of these endangered creatures and preserve its species. All the chameleon species including the Pygmy Leaf are all protected under international laws and these laws should be abide to ensure the stability of the species' population.

Like any other animal species such as birds, snakes or common pets like dogs and cats, illegal pet trading is a big problem because it has a huge impact in conservation issues. If you don't have the time, expertise, and money to take care of these endangered creatures, it may be better to turn them over to experts or wildlife authorities. The chameleons you will catch in the wild or near your area needs to be raised properly. For first time handlers it's highly recommended that you purchase one that is bred in captivity or those who are newly hatched.

Pygmy Leaf Chameleons and Other Pets

Pygmy leaf chameleon or chameleons in general can get along with other chameleon breed with no more than one male in an enclosure, as long as there is enough space and vegetation, adequate living environment, and peaceful surroundings they can definitely co-exist with other species of their own kind. It may not be advisable or even wise to introduce them to other house pets. As mentioned earlier, these creatures because of its small size are always threatened, and if introducing them to other pets or even being randomly exposed to strangers may not be a good idea. Their defense mechanism such as vibrating and camouflage may disturb any pet or friends. You certainly don't want these delicate creatures to feel threatened because you may not see them for who they really are.

Exposing them to strangers or other pets may also affect their health and behavior. It may cause certain diseases or may even shorten their lives.

Ease and Cost of Care

Even if these creatures are small and manageable, owning and maintaining one still doesn't come cheap! The fact is that, these chameleons require maintenance which means that you have to provide supplies and be able to cover the expenses in order for you to maintain a healthy lifestyle and environment for your pet.

These things will definitely add up to your daily budget, and the cost will vary depending on where you purchase it; the brand of the materials, the nutrients included in its food and the time being. If you want to seriously own a pygmy leaf chameleon as a pet you should be able to cover the necessary costs it entails.

In this section you will receive an overview of the expenses associated with purchasing and keeping a pygmy leaf chameleon such as its vivarium, supplements, lighting, watering and veterinary care. You will receive an overview of these costs as well as an estimate for each in the following pages of this section.

Overall Costs

The overall costs for keeping a pygmy leaf chameleon include those costs that you must cover before you can bring your chameleon home. Some of the costs you will need to cover include you're the enclosure or cage, food and water equipment, supplies and cage décor or accessories, breeding materials, medical care - not to mention the cost of the pygmy leaf chameleon itself. It is highly recommended that you buy from online stores or websites, legit breeders as well as during any reptile conventions, or even find vivarium equipment in hardware or fixture stores because the products and materials are a lot cheaper than if you purchase everything from a pet store.

You will find an overview of each of these costs as well as an estimate for each below:

Purchase Price: $20 - $38 (for pairs)

The cost to purchase a pygmy leaf chameleon can vary greatly depending on the breed, its age, and your local area. You can probably find a backyard breeder offering $20 or below, but you cannot be sure of the breeding quality for these chameleons. Generally speaking, pet-quality pygmy leaf chameleon sells for $20 and up. Buying from legit breeders during a reptile convention may neither be cheap or expensive.

Baby and Adult Enclosures: $30 - $300

When you purchase a chameleon, you need to make sure that its vivarium or terrarium are somewhat similar to its natural habitat in the wild, so that it won't have trouble adjusting to its new environment. Providing adequate shelter will make them feel at ease and comfortable as a house pet. They may need to get used to you or other people checking them out while they are inside their enclosure so make sure that the kind of cage you will buy will protect them from any dangerous threats around the house including your house pets.

Terrariums even though it may be quite time consuming in terms of cleaning it, is much suitable for your pygmy leaf chameleon because it will provide ample air circulation than aquariums. While many owners discouraged using glass enclosures, it might still come in handy during extreme weather conditions or climate for those living in extremely dry or cold countries. You can also opt to create a D-I-Y or Do – it – Yourself cage using alternative materials like wood; it could be a great alternative if you would want to have a cheaper enclosure. Wooden cage materials may cost $50 or less.

Lighting and Gauges: $50 and up

Adequate lighting will provide appropriate heat temperature inside your chameleon's terrarium or cage enclosure. You need to purchase things like a UVB bulb, heat bulb and light fixtures as well.

Gauges is also helpful to easily control temperatures and the cage's humidity levels.

Food, Supplements, Watering: total of approx: $150

Aside from buying food like live insects, veggies, and other gut loading foods you need to also provide supplements for your chameleon, this is equivalent to vitamins for us humans to protect them against diseases and strengthen the body. You also need to install a watering system for your pet. You can use a spray bottle or dripper which is much cheaper or you can opt to buy an automatic misting system but it's much more expensive.

Veterinarian Consultations: $100 - $200

Like humans, or any other pets, these cute reptiles do get sick and most often than not once you find out it's already worst or an emergency case already. Be sure to save up for its medical needs and vet costs. You may also need to do some medical checkups and/or lab tests once in a while for your pet.

Supplies/Accessories: average of $50 - $100

In addition to purchasing your pygmy leaf chameleon's enclosure and installing fixtures, you should also purchase cage decors such as branches, leaves, live plants and other accessories to ensure that they'll live in a familiar habitat. You also need to buy a laying bin if in case you'd be breeding a chameleon. The bin for female chameleons can be quite expensive. The cost for these items will vary depending on the quality and also quantity, so you should budget about $50 - $100 or more for these extra costs.

Expenses Overview

Needs	Costs
Purchase Price	$20 - $38 (£16.06 - £30.52)
Baby/Adult Enclosures	$30 - $300 (£24.10 - £240.96)
Lighting and Gauges	$50 (£40.16)
Food, Supplements, Watering	$150 (£120.48)
Vet Consultations	$100 to $200 (£80.32 - £160.64)
Supplies/Accessories	$50 - $100 (£40.16 - £80.32)
Total	$400 to $838 (£321.28 – £673.08)

*Costs may vary depending on location
**Costs may change based on the currency exchange

Pros and Cons of Pygmy Leaf Chameleons

Before you bring a pygmy leaf chameleon home you should take the time to learn the pros and cons of the breed. Every chameleon breed is different so you need to think about the details to determine whether a pygmy leaf chameleon is actually the right pet for you.

In this section you will find a list of pros and cons for pygmy leaf chameleon specie:

Pros for Pygmy Leaf Chameleon:

- A pet that doesn't need to interact constantly with owners
- A pet that is satisfied and happy inside its enclosure or terrarium
- A pet that has the ability to easily adapt to its environment
- A pet that doesn't require exercises or training
- A pet that is very easy to handle (although most of the time it's not necessary)
- A pet that has no special needs unlike popular or high – energy pets that demands attention

Cons for Pygmy Leaf Chameleon:

- Has a very short lifespan
- May require some attention
- May come across as boring or non – interactive
- Cannot be handled all the time
- Quite sensitive and delicate
- Not advisable for first time owners

Can be quite expensive in terms of its habitat needs

Chapter Three: Tips in Buying Pygmy Leaf Chameleons

Now that you are already aware and have prior knowledge about the legal aspects of owning and maintaining a Pygmy Leaf Chameleon as well as its pros and cons, the next step is purchasing one through a legitimate breeder or during reptile conventions. In this chapter you will find valuable information about where to find a pygmy leaf chameleon breeder, how to quarantine them, and how to differentiate a healthy pygmy leaf chameleon from an unhealthy one.

Where to Purchase a Pygmy Leaf Chameleons

It is best that you only purchase a captive bred chameleon. It may cost you a little extra dollars but it is worth it because you will be assured that your chameleon is healthy and doesn't have any illnesses or transmitted diseases. Aside from that it will also benefit captive breeding programs, and will help them to further breed healthy chameleons in the future.

If you choose to buy from a backyard breeder, you may not be certain about its health, and these chameleons that are caught in the wild may be endangered already. You may risk from the issues of importation damages – these are animals that are illegally imported from the wild every year and are usually in poor health condition. These wild chameleons may also have difficulty in adjusting to a captive life. It is also not recommended that you buy from local pet stores because most of it is only selling chameleons for profit and most often than not some of these creatures are in poor condition because they are living in an unhealthy environment.

The needs of chameleons in general are overlooked by pet stores, and if you buy from them for the sole reason that you want to rescue the animal from an inadequate environment, the store will only replace it or re-stock it with another chameleon without investing in proper care, and without improving environmental conditions, that is why it is better if you give your money to legitimate captive breeding programs.

Before purchasing you should also first identify if the chameleon or pygmy leaf chameleon is a captive breed or caught in the wild. Another important tip is to verify with the seller or provider the kind of species or the kind of chameleon you are purchasing. Most of the time, chameleons on sale are mislabeled so make sure that you are getting the appropriate species so you can also give it the appropriate care.

If your provider is unsure then you may ask a reputable source or an expert in chameleons to identify the kind of breed you want to buy.

Aside from local pet stores, legitimate breeders, and reptile conventions, you can also get referrals on where you can purchase a healthy pygmy leaf chameleon from several forums online or online communities. These communities usually have contacts, has history information regarding responsible breeding, and you can also get ideas on how to properly care for your new pet chameleon.

Important Reminder:

You should only purchase baby chameleons that are 2 – 3 month old already. Sure you can buy a baby pygmy chameleon but it may not be suitable for first time owners. Baby chameleons are very delicate and fragile; you'll have more chance of successfully raising a much older chameleon. Beware of breeders or hobbyists who are selling chameleons that are too young.

Quarantine

Reptiles in general, and chameleons in particular whether they are caught from the wild or breed in captivity should be quarantined for at least 45 days.

Quarantining your pygmy leaf chameleon should be strictly done in order for you to assess the health of your pet and to make sure that it is not a carrier of transmittable disease to prevent from transferring it to you, your other pets or your family.

The main reason for this specifically for chameleons is that these creatures do not show any signs of illnesses and can hold on to it for a long time without being noticed. The environmental stresses of shipping, traveling or being in a new habitat can trigger a hidden ailment. If you do not quarantine a pet, it can expose your other pets to potentially infectious or viral diseases.

Here are some steps you need to take for a successful quarantine period for your pygmy leaf chameleon:

- Put your new Pygmy Leaf chameleon in a separate room, away from your other pets or chameleons for at least 45 days.

- Make sure to feed and handle all your other pets before introducing or placing the newly quarantine chameleon with them to avoid contamination.

- Make sure to use separate equipment for the quarantine chameleon, and always wash your hands after handling them.

- Cage hygiene should always be done to prevent the spread of germs or parasites. The reason for this is that new imported chameleons have intestinal parasites. Constantly cleaning and furnishing will help avoid these problems.

- It is highly recommended that you test your new pet's fecal sample at your vet for diagnosis and testing.

Choosing a Reputable Breeder

To make sure that you get a well-bred, healthy and robust pygmy leaf chameleon, your best bet is to look around for a legitimate breeder. Feel free to ask around at the various chameleon forums online and you may also be able to get a personal recommendation from friends or your local veterinarian. Once you have your list of breeders on hand you can go through them one-by-one to narrow down your options.

Here are the following guidelines for you to be able to choose a reputable pygmy leaf chameleon breeder:

Do a Background Check on the Breeder

Visit the website for each breeder on your list (if they have one) and look for key information about the breeder's history and experience.

- Check for licenses or document registrations to ensure the legitimacy of the breeder, if applicable.

- If the website doesn't provide any information about the facilities or the breeder you are best just moving on.

Interview the Breeders

Now that you have narrowed down some breeders, contact the remaining breeders on your list by phone

- Ask the breeder questions about his experience with breeding chameleons in general and about the specific pygmy leaf chameleon breed you are looking for.
- Ask for information about the breeding stock including registration and health information (if they have any).

- Expect a reputable breeder to ask you questions about yourself as well – a responsible breeder wants to make sure that his chameleons go to good homes.

Do an Onsite Inspection

Schedule an appointment to visit the facilities for the remaining breeders on your list after you've weeded a few of them out.

- Ask for a tour of the facilities, including the place where the chameleon collections are kept.

- If the surroundings look unorganized or unclean, do not purchase from the breeder or from the local pet store.

- Make sure the collections is in good condition and that the pygmy leaf chameleon are all healthy - looking and active.

Characteristics of a Reputable Breeder

By this time you should have narrowed down the best of the best breeders on your list, before making a decision consider every factor to make the most out of it. Make sure the breeder provides some kind of health guarantee and ask about any medical information the pygmy leaf chameleons may already have. Below are some characteristics you should look out for when selecting a reputable breeder.

- The breeder should be willing to educate or explain and answer all your questions expertly.

- The breeder should allow on - site visits, however if you are far from the place, you should be able to request photos or videos from the breeder and he/she should gladly show them to you so that you won't waste your time.

- The breeder should offer a contract and some sort of warranty.

- The breeder should be willing to take back or rehome the chameleon regardless of the situation.

- The breeder should allow you to reach him/her before and after purchasing the pygmy leaf chameleon.

- The breeder should be able to provide health records and also have contacts with veterinarian as well as firsthand information about the pygmy leaf chameleon's overall health

- The breeder should also explain to you the risks or the cons of keeping one as a pet not just its advantages.

- The breeder should be transparent and honest about how they raised and bred chameleons so that you'll know that they're reputable and a caring owner as well.

List of Breeders and Rescue Websites

There are so many chameleons to choose from, that's why you need to do some research and decide which breed you want before you start shopping around. When you are ready to buy a pygmy leaf chameleon, you then need to start thinking about where you are going to get it. You may be able to find a pygmy leaf chameleon at some local breeders near your area, but think carefully before you buy whether that is really the best option. Follow the quick guidelines mentioned earlier to ensure the quality of its breeding.

If you want a baby pygmy leaf chameleon, you can probably find some at rescue websites, you may also try adopting a pygmy leaf chameleon from a reputable breeder as well, or purchase from the exerts at reptile convention events, who knows it might be the better option for you.

Here is the list of breeders and websites that sell pygmy leaf chameleons:

Breeders and Rescue Websites

Back Water Reptiles
<http://www.backwaterreptiles.com/chameleons/pygmy-chameleon-for-sale.html>

FL Chams
<http://flchams.com/chameleons/pygmy-chameleons-for-sale/>

LLL Reptile
<https://www.lllreptile.com/locations>

Tarantula Spiders (includes other reptiles)
<http://tarantulaspiders.com/Weekly_Price_List.php>

Reptile City
<http://www.reptilecity.com/Merchant2/merchant.mvc?Screen=PROD&Product_Code=PC>

Underground Reptiles
<https://undergroundreptiles.com/product-category/animals/lizards/chameleons/>

Fauna Classifieds
<http://www.faunaclassifieds.com/forums/showthread.php?p=1695690>

Exotic – Pets UK
<https://www.exotic-pets.co.uk/chameleons-for-sale.html>

Pets Classifieds UK
<http://www.pets-classifieds.co.uk/ps_pygmy+chameleons.php>

Pearl Trees
<http://www.pearltrees.com/t/chameleons/id5343123#1349>

ReptilesNCritters
<http://www.reptilesncritters.com/leaf-pygmy-chameleons.html>

First Choice Reptiles

<http://www.firstchoicereptiles.com/chameleons-for-sale/>

Selecting a Healthy Pygmy Leaf Chameleons

As mentioned earlier selecting a healthy chameleon will save you from a lot of headaches and vet bills in the long run. If you are a first time chameleon owner, it is best to start off with a healthy one because an ill chameleon can be very challenging to the inexperienced. Chameleons are the kind of animals that do not show any signs of diseases for a long time without being noticed. It's imperative that before purchasing one you should look for basic signs of a healthy pygmy leaf chameleon.

After you have narrowed down your list of options to just two or three pygmy leaf chameleon breeders, your next step is to actually pick out the chameleon you want. You have already determined that the remaining breeders on your list are responsible, but now you need to make sure that the pygmy leaf chameleon they have available are healthy and ready to go home with you

Here are some few guidelines to keep in mind when selecting a healthy pygmy leaf chameleon:

Signs of a Healthy Chameleon:

- A healthy chameleon should be active in its environment and standing up rather than lying on its perch.
- The chameleon should be able to move about the cage with good balance without falling or stumbling.
- The eyes should be full, open at all times and actively looking all around.
- The arm and leg bones should all be straight, toes should all be intact and the chameleon should have a strong grip.
- The chameleon's skin should have vibrant coloration all over the body and all the spines on the back should be present.
- Patches of shedding skin should be normal if present.
- The tail should be able to grasp branches and curl up smoothly.

Signs of an Unhealthy Chameleon:

- A chameleon that sleeps during the day.
- It has sunken or swollen eyes.
- If it is lying on the bottom of the cage.
- Legs that are bent, curved, appear to have multiple joints or have swellings at the joints.

- Wrinkly, crusty or dry skin, bumps, cuts or bruises, or patches of abnormal colored skin.
- Blood at the mouth, swollen jaw, or jaw that doesn't align properly.
- A tail that cannot curl or is black at the end.
- If your chameleon is falling off branches, having a weak grip, stumbling or appearing very clumsy.

Chapter Four: Habitat for Your Pygmy Leaf Chameleons

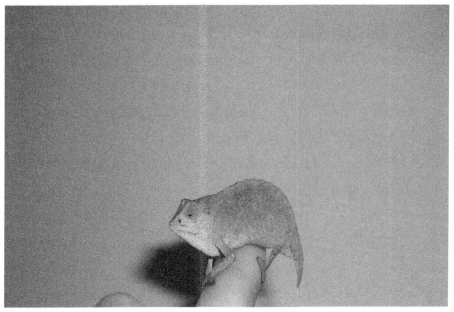

The Pygmy Leaf Chameleon makes an awesome pet largely because of its very docile personality, although these chameleons can easily adjust and adapt to a new living condition, it may still be quite challenging especially for chameleons caught in the wild. You may want to make your new pet as comfortable as it can be so that it can get used to its new home, and to also avoid being stressed out.

In this chapter you will learn the basics about your Pygmy Leaf chameleon's habitat requirements including on how to set up its cage, useful accessories, and some things to avoid when it comes to setting up its enclosure or terrarium.

Habitat Requirements for Pygmy Leaf Chameleons

Unlike other pets, pygmy leaf chameleon doesn't need too much space to roam around with. It's one of the major advantages of having this creature as a pet because they are low maintenance in terms of its habitat requirements compared to larger animals or common pets such as dogs or cats. But aside from space, the main thing your pygmy leaf chameleon needs in terms of its habitat is lots of love and affection from his human companions and be able to provide adequate living condition. Pygmy leaf chameleons may not be the kind of breed that bonds closely with family (although it can be one!), but just like any other pets you should make an effort to spend some quality time with your pet chameleon each and every day. If your pygmy leaf doesn't get enough attention it may more likely to develop several behavioral problems that can affect its health as well.

In addition to building its habitat requirements, you also need to add other terrarium accessories not just for aesthetic purposes but mainly for the purpose of resembling the chameleon's habitat or environment in the wild. You should also keep in mind some things you should avoid when it comes to creating its terrarium which will be discussed later on in this chapter.

Keep reading to learn the basics about your pygmy leaf chameleon's habitat requirements. You will be given tips and guidelines on how to create and maintain an ideal habitat for your pet chameleon.

Ideal Habitat for Pygmy Leaf Chameleon

As mentioned earlier in this book, you need to house your pet chameleon in an enclosure or a terrarium because aside from its size, its ability to change colors or shades, and the fact that they are quite sensitive creatures, they are mostly an observation kind of pet.

- **Cage Size**

The rule of thumb when it comes to building or purchasing an enclosure for your chameleon is that the size or space should at least be 5 gallons for each pygmy leaf. Of course you need to adjust accordingly if you plan on keeping lots of chameleons in an enclosure.

It is more preferred that the cage is wide or has a horizontal space instead of a vertical one because some chameleons can't climb that high. Although some experts think otherwise; nevertheless the ideal cage size that will balance this issue out should be 18"x18"x36" (45cm x 45 cm x 91cm). Just don't make the mistake of creating or buying a cage that is too small.

For pygmy leaf chameleons, experts recommend that you purchase a glass cage like an aquarium simply because it can easily be planted with branches, and you can also landscaped its bottom part to make it look like a forest floor.

Pygmy leaf chameleons or chameleons in general can co - exist with each other and they can be housed communally; although male chameleons should not be housed together unless the cage is huge enough (over 40 gallons).

Keep in mind though that your chameleon collections should not feel stressed out by the presence of its other occupants. You should also make sure that there are lots of hiding places, lots of branches (for exercise/climbing opportunities) and lots of plants inside.

- **Plants and Branches**

We all know that chameleons love to hide their true colors, or identity. In the wild it is a defense mechanism so that they can't be eaten by predators, but in captivity especially if they're around their own kind; it's more of a unique ability, and a form of stimulation.

In line with this, you should be able to provide lots of branches and plants or leaves as well as hiding places or areas for your pygmy leaf chameleons because that will enable them to practice their natural ability, make them feel comfortable in their new home, and will also make them feel close to their natural habitat even in captivity.

Try adding green or brown leaves (fresh or fake) because it will make your chameleon feel safe, and if they feel secure you can most likely see them out of their hiding places, and be able to observe them.

You can use both fake and real live plants; live plants can help increase as well as maintain humidity inside the enclosure. Another advantage of using real plants is that it can also hold water droplets for drinking, and if ever your pygmy leaf chameleon decides to eat it, it will be edible and safe. It's highly recommended that you use real plants.

Keep in mind to only use non – toxic plants so that the feeder bugs could also eat them. The most commonly used plants in chameleon enclosures are Hibiscus, Schefflera arboricola, Ficus, and Pothos. If you buy a plant from the pet store you may not be sure if it is safe for your chameleon due to insecticides and toxic fertilizers that could affect your pet just make sure to properly wash them with soap and water to remove harmful chemical residues.

Make sure to repot the top ½ of the soil with organic soil and cover any soil with large rocks or screen because your chameleon could ingest soil causing impactions. Keep in mind to also wash all the leaves first before putting them inside to rinse off any chemical residues that could be poisonous for your pygmy leaf.

Aside from plants, chameleons also need to have an adequate exercise; in the wild these creatures always go from one branch to another, they love to climb branches of plants that is around them. This is why you need to purchase branches as well as vines because it will also provide them stimulation. Small wires can be used to hold and secure the vines and branches in place.

Make sure to clean the small branches if you're going to grab one from outside plants. Also wash the bake branches before using it. You can buy bendy vines at various pet stores - they also make a great cage décor.

For the perches you can use dowels, fishing line, garbage bag ties, colorful push pins or thumb tacks to secure it. The more creative you are the better!

You may also want to arrange, and re - arrange the branch, vines and plant settings from time to time. The top zone of the cage should be used for basking, while the lower zone should be for relaxing, and hunting or cooling off for you to make the most out of the cage's space, and for your pet to feel safe, comfortable and happy with its surroundings.

Remember that a great living condition can improve your chameleon's health and overall lifespan.

Cage Setup Guidelines

There are many ways on how to set up a great habitat for your pygmy leaf chameleon, but aside from the materials used for its cage, you also need to include equipment to sustain an adequate living condition for these animals. Below are some general guidelines you should follow when installing these equipment.

- **UVB light/ Lighting Fixtures**

Every cage or enclosure should have one UVB light as well as one basking light for appropriate wattage. It's important that the lights be placed on top and it is outside the cage with the light shining downwards. The UVB light bulb (Reptisun 5.0 linear fluorescent) must also be replaced every 6 – 8 months, and the heat bulb (40 – 60 watts) should also be replaced once it burns out.

For the lighting fixtures, you should opt to buy a linear fluorescent fixture and also a spotlight fixture used for the heat bulb. It's always available in hardware or home improvement stores. It's also highly recommended that you purchase an automatic timer for the lighting.

- **Screens and Ventilation**

There should be a screen on top of the cage simply because UVB rays cannot penetrate plastic or glass. The screen cages should also have good ventilation. You should also adjust the ventilation based on the kind of cage you purchase for your chameleon and your geographic location as well.

Things to Avoid Inside the Cage

- **Waterfall**

Reptile waterfalls should not be used inside the cage because it harbors molds and bacteria which are not safe for drinking. The only watering equipment that must be used for your chameleon is drippers for misting.

- **Water Bowl**

Chameleons should not be drinking from water bowls because aside from bacterial growth, it can also drown them since they are miniature in size. In the forest, chameleons usually drink from rain drops on the leaves and trees that is why it is recommended to only use a dripper so that they can drink from the accumulated water droplets on the leaves or plants inside their cage.

- **Heat Rocks**

Pygmy leaf chameleons are arboreal reptiles which mean that they are tree - dwelling species, they are not ground dwellers or they don't seek a warm rock for basking like lizards. Using heat rocks or ground heaters can easily burn their feet and belly. Don't ever use heat pads or heat rocks.

- **Light bulbs that are inside cage**

Chameleons love to climb and crawl that's why they can easily reach the top of their cage where most heating and lighting equipment are attached. It's important that you don't put the light bulbs or any lighting fixtures inside their cage because it can easily burn them and it's not safe.

Chapter Five: Feeding Your Pygmy Leaf Chameleon

Meeting your Pygmy Leaf chameleon's nutritional needs is very important to ensure that your pet stays healthy, and strong against diseases. Every kind of chameleon species have different nutritional requirements, that's why reading this chapter is important because it will focus only on pygmy chameleon breeds. Chameleons, like many other pets, should be given the right amount of recommended food for a balanced nutrition because proper diet can also lengthen the short life expectancy of your pet.

In this section, you'll learn the majority of your pet's nutritional needs; tips on how to feed them as well as recommended foods that are good for their health and foods to avoid.

Nutritional Needs of Pygmy Leaf Chameleons

Chameleons in general are insectivores which mean that they should only be fed live insects. You can easily tell if your pygmy leaf is hunting for food because its head is facing down at the bottom of the cage or enclosure. Pygmy leaf chameleons love to eat cricket, baby silkworms, and baby hornworms. The general rule of thumb is to only feed insects that are not longer than the width of your chameleon's head. The length of the insects should ideally be 1/8 to 1/4 inches.

Feeding Amount for Pygmy Leaf:

- Neonates (0 to 3 months): feed them as many fruit flies or pinhead crickets as they can eat several times a day.

- Juveniles: (3 - 6 months): feed them around 6 - 10 small crickets daily.

- Adults: feed them 4 - 6 small crickets every other day

Gut - load

Gut loading of food is a kind of process where you increase the nutritional value of the insects that you feed to your pygmy leaf chameleon. The concept is very simple, since we all live in an ecosystem, we all benefit from one another in various ways. A great example is the eagle, eagles eat snakes, while snakes eat rodents or chickens, chickens feed on worms, and worms feed in various sources. It is same with chameleons in the wild, their insect preys also feed on many different nutrition sources within that ecosystem, which makes balance nutrition. However, in captivity, it's just impossible to create that kind of natural cycle, so in order to replicate that you as the owner should properly gut load the food that you feed your chameleons.

You need to also properly feed the insects or the prey a special diet or good nutrition so that in the end your chameleon will benefit from that very balanced and proper nutrition.

In order for you to gut load the food of your pygmy leaf chameleon you should supplement it with a multivitamin powder with calcium. The calcium should be higher than phosphorus, because high phosphorus inhibits calcium absorption. The supplements should also be low in oxalates.

Unfortunately, most commercial gut loads are low in calcium which may not be sufficient for your chameleon's nutritional needs. The great thing is that you can actually create a Do – It – Yourself gut load that contains the needed nutrients for your pet at home. It's very easy to make and quite inexpensive.

Here are the following tips on how to create your own gut load:

- Get at least two or three options (either fruits or vegetables) from the store in which you can use as gut load to your chameleon's food, and then just rotate them every now and then.

- Always wash all the produce to rinse off any pesticide or chemical residues; peel the fruit's skin cover or cut the veggies because sometimes the pesticide or chemical components stick to the fruit or vegetable.

- The time wherein you should feed your insects to your pygmy leaf chameleon should be no more than 12 hours from the time you gut load it.

Primary Gut – loading Ingredients

The following suggested ingredients should be the primary component of your gut load. They are high in calcium, low in oxalates, phosphorus, and goitrogens.

- Mustard greens
- Dandelion leaves
- Turnip Greens
- Collard Greens
- Papaya
- Escarole Lettuce
- Watercress
- Alfalfa

Secondary Gut – loading Ingredients

The following suggested ingredients are only secondary components for your gut load. They are only moderately high in calcium, has a relatively low oxalates, phosphorus, and goitrogens components. They are additional ingredients for your gut – load.

- Sweet Potato
- Carrots
- Butternut
- Mango

- Orange
- Kale
- Apples
- Squash
- Beet Greens
- Bok Choy
- Blackberries
- Green beans

Dry Gut – loading Ingredients:

The primary and secondary ingredients can also be mixed with dry gut load and homemade mixes for a well – rounded nutrition.

- Sunflower seeds (organic and non – salted)
- Bee pollen
- Dried Seaweed
- Spirulina
- Flax seed
- Almonds (organic and non – salted)

Toxic Gut – loading Ingredients

The following suggested ingredients should be avoided and must not be included in your gut - load. They are very low in calcium, and high in phosphorus, oxalates, and goitrogens.

- Cabbage
- Potatoes
- Iceberg Lettuce
- Romain Lettuce
- Spinach
- Broccoli
- Tomatoes
- Grains
- Corns
- Vertebrates (pinkies, lizards etc.)
- Oats
- Beans
- Meat
- Eggs
- Cereals
- Cat food/ Dog Food
- Fish food
- Canned/ dead insects

Important Reminder:

You should never let your pygmy leaf chameleon eat vertebrates such as lizards because first of all it's not even part of their normal diet even in the wild. If you feed them meat or a carnivore diet, it will surely damage their kidneys and gout due to the difference in protein breakdown. Only feed your chameleon an all – insect diet plus good gut loaded ingredients and supplementation.

Supplementation

Calcium is very important to your pygmy leaf chameleons diet as well as vitamins that can be found in powdered supplements. You should sprinkle a small amount of these powdered supplements in the feeder insect before giving them to your pygmy leaf chameleon. Use calcium twice a week, as well as calcium with D3 and a multivitamin at least once a month.

Hydration & Misting

Your chameleon's cage should be misted twice a day and dry it out completely. The purpose of this is to raise relative humidity so that it will encourage your pygmy leaf chameleon to drink. Be reminded to not use water bowls or any water standing source because they won't recognize that, they only drink from the droplets of water found in leaves or in plants.

Feeding Tips

Below are some feeding tips you can easily follow and implement when feeding your Pygmy Leaf Chameleon:

- Feed you chameleon on the first half of the day (usually in the morning) so that they can digest their food and will have enough time to bask properly.

- If you are feeding crickets to your Pygmy Leaf chameleon, you should first gut loaded it with calcium enriched vegetables few hours before feeding them to your chameleon.

- Keep in mind that inadequate dietary calcium leads to metabolic bone disease, a very serious and potentially fatal chameleon illness.

Chapter Six: Pygmy Leaf Chameleon Husbandry

Chapter 4 have already given you an idea on how to build a cage, the materials needed for an enclosure, as well as the equipment that need to be installed, this time you will be given in depth and technical information on how to keep your pygmy leaf chameleon happy while it is inside its habitat. You will learn husbandry tips including the proper amount of lighting, setting up the heat temperature as well as adjusting levels of humidity. This will help maintain a good environmental condition for your chameleon.

Temperature

The temperature for Pygmy Leaf chameleon inside its cage should be 15 – 25 degrees Celsius or 60 – 78 degrees Fahrenheit. Don't ever set the temperature over 26 degrees Celsius or 80 degrees Fahrenheit this high temperature is fatal.

Humidity

Another important aspect of chameleon husbandry is the humidity. Pygmy leaf chameleons require around 60 – 80% humidity, this can be achieved by conducting misting sessions in the enclosure every day. The advantage of live plants is that it increases and also maintains humidity levels. It is also highly recommended if you have the budget to purchase a time – controlled misting system or a cool mist humidifier.

You have to always make sure that the humidity inside the enclosure is just set at a right temperature; you don't want to dehydrate your pygmy leaf because it can be a factor in getting an MBD or the Metabolic Bone Disease. Sometimes it can be very humid or too cold inside because the temperature outside depending on the geographical location also vary, to make sure that the humidity level is just right, you can use some form of ventilation by providing a small fan, similar to a computer fan inside the CPU so that the air can properly circulate around the cage. However, keep in mind that the fan must not be too powerful otherwise it could mess up with the thermal gradient.

Proper ventilation will provide a good airflow around the enclosure which will help in reducing fungal growth, and making sure that the enclosure will not overheat especially during summer or hot days. A good airflow will also benefit the growth of live plants inside the terrarium.

Lighting

As mentioned in the previous chapters, lighting is needed because even if pygmy leaf chameleons or chameleons in general doesn't like to be exposed to the sun too much they still need like most of us Vitamin D which we can get from the sun's rays. Of course you can't just leave the enclosure outside so that your pet could get an authentic sunlight, that's why you will need to purchase and install a 2.0 or 5.0 UVB bulb that is low intensity. This bulb is usually good for only 6 months after which it needs to be replaced.

You might also need a basking bulb for your pygmy leaf. This bulb acts as a heat gradient that will allow your cold – blooded chameleon to be able to regulate its body temperature. You pygmy leaf chameleon then can assess if it needs to move to warmer or cooler areas inside the enclosure.

Just make sure that it doesn't exceed 26C (80F) degrees. Keep in mind that the UVB light must be on for about 12 hours, and also provide 12 hours of darkness inside the cage so that your pygmy leaf chameleons can rest. It will serve as their day and night period.

Chapter Seven: Breeding Your Pygmy Leaf Chameleon

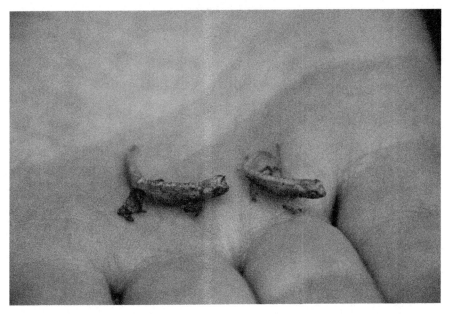

If keeping a Pygmy Leaf Chameleon is already challenging enough for you especially for first time owners, you might just want to stick to becoming an expert at it for a while before deciding to breed more of them. This chapter is may not be suitable for everyone, even if you are already a chameleon owner. Handling and breeding female Pygmy leaf chameleons can be quite challenging and it can take much of your time. Breeding can be difficult because these creatures are quite delicate and very sensitive, however if you think you're up for the challenge, or would just want to know how breeding works, the information in this chapter can be useful for you. Read on!

Breeding Basics

Pygmy chameleons unlike other larger breeds of chameleons can be kept within the same cage at all times even if their mate is with them. Courtship between a male and a female pygmy leaf is as simple as the male nodding its head at the female pygmy.

Usually female chameleons don't display a different coloration or shade, but its natural color will be rather visible as it gets closer to giving birth. You may not need a laying bin but the enclosure must contain a few inches of substrate or organic soil at the floor of the cage. Some of the substrate should be a bit wet or moist because this is where chameleons usually lay their eggs.

You can't actually see the female chameleons giving birth or building its nest because aside from their miniature size, and all their "invisibility" abilities, they are just plain secretive. They usually give birth behind the plants and leaves scattered around the enclosure or in the hidden spaces you built for them. However, if you happen to see your female chameleon appears thinner or has gotten slimmer than it used to be that's usually a sign that she has given birth.

If you can find the location where the eggs are buried or tucked away, you should immediately incubate it; carefully removed the eggs because they are micro – small, and incubate it at 18 – 25 degrees Celsius or 65 – 78F. You can put the eggs in a sealed container or inside a cabinet if the temperature is right. It will take about 45 – 90 days before the eggs hatch. The eggs sizes will get larger as they get closer to cracking up or hatching.

Raising Baby Pygmy Leaf Chameleons

Neonates or newly born chameleons should be removed from the cage if they were not incubated artificially because predation is what usually happens. Mothers eating their newly born babies are an animal's natural instinct.

Neonates can co – exist inside a similar cage where their other sibling pygmy leaf chameleons are as long as it is in a similar 5 gallon cage size. The bottom part of the cage should be left bare, and it should contain artificial plants as well as mini branches where neonates can climb or hide as well.

The proper temperature should not be over 24 degrees Celsius or 76 degrees Fahrenheit. You may also want to add UVB light, it's not required but it is optional and also recommended so that your new baby pygmies can also receive appropriate heat.

Similar to the typical adult pygmy leaf chameleons, the cage of your neonates should be well misted at least multiple times in one day. Your new hatchlings should also be fed flightless fruit flies as much as they can eat in a day. You can also dust these fruit flies with calcium (at least once a week) or what we call gut – loading so that your new baby chameleons can receive supplements and have a balanced and healthy nutrition.

The males and female newly born siblings should be separated by around 3 to 4 months. You can differentiate a male from a female by its tail lengths although it may not be accurate. Ask your vet if you want to know how to identify their sex.

Chapter Eight: Keeping Your Chameleon Healthy

Once you've bought a healthy Pygmy Leaf chameleon, you must know how to keep it healthy. What do they need? How much should you feed them? What are the symptoms of possible diseases? You should be able to tell when your pygmy leaf chameleon needs a trip to the vet. In this chapter, you will be given information about the potential illnesses that could threaten your chameleon's health. Having an idea and information about these diseases can make you be aware of its potential threats and be able to prevent it before it affects your pet chameleon.

Common Health Problems

Chameleons can be affected by a number of different health problems and they are generally not specific to any particular breed. Feeding your pygmy leaf a nutritious diet will go a long way in securing his total health and well - being, but sometimes chameleons get ill anyway. If you want to make sure that your reptile gets the treatment he needs as quickly as possible you need to learn how to identify the symptoms of disease. These symptoms are not always obvious either; your pygmy leaf may not show any outward signs of illness except for a subtle change in behavior. As mentioned many time before in previous chapters, chameleons do not show any physical signs until it's too late most of the time.

The more time you spend with your pet chameleon, the more you will come to understand its behavior – this is the key to catching health problems early. At the first sign that something is wrong with your pet you should take inventory of his symptoms – both physical and behavioral – so you can relay them to your veterinarian who will then make a diagnosis and prescribe a course of treatment. The sooner you identify these symptoms, the sooner your vet can take action and the more likely your pygmy leaf chameleon will be able to make a full recovery.

Pygmy leaf can be prone to a wide variety of different diseases or infections, though some are more common than others. For the benefit your pygmy leaf's long-term health, take the time to learn the causes, symptoms, and treatment options for some of the most common health problems.

Besides red flags, it is best to be in the know when it comes to what these red flags mean. Pygmy leaf chameleons have some common health issues you can find by identifying the symptoms or causes. Here are some of the common health issues to look out for:

Dehydration

Dehydration is one of the leading health issues among chameleons. The very obvious symptom is sunken eyes although it can also be caused by other health problems. Aside from sunken eyes, symptoms also include orange urates, sunken head (pads), and sudden weight loss. The best way to avoid dehydration for your chameleon is to increase misting schedule, make sure to maintain the appropriate humidity and also give your pet access to drippers because it can help in improving their hydration and make them frequent drinkers. You can also use showers as long as it is properly supervised or controlled, it can help simulate a rain. If your chameleon is always dehydrated it can lead to potential serious illnesses in the long run. Make sure that your chameleon always goes to a reptile vet if such symptoms don't improve.

Metabolic Bone Disease (MBD)

The Metabolic Bone Disease is the most common disease among reptiles in general. This disease is caused by a lack in dietary calcium, improper lighting, and also imbalanced nutrition.

As mentioned earlier in the feeding chapter of the book, your chameleon should have the right amount of calcium and must eat food that is low in phosphorous. If the calcium levels are low, the body will be forced to get calcium source straight from the bones so that there will be enough energy for the body to function especially for muscle movements and metabolism. The effect however is that the bones becomes weak and eventually brittle. This disease is very painful and definitely fatal for chameleons.

The usual signs you should look out for is bent leg bones, double elbows, stunted growth, decrease in the use of its tongue, double knees, misaligned mouth, soft jaw or if you it grabbing its own limbs or head.

If your chameleon gets affected with MBD it cannot be reversed but the good news is that the process of progression of the disease can be stopped. If prevented, the bones can be treated with proper medications, and it can heal over time. Proper husbandry such as enough access to UVB lighting as well as proper nutrition can correct the calcium imbalance in the body. This is why bringing your chameleon to the vet once you see any early signs of Metabolic Bone Disease can be very helpful and lifesaving; it can stop further bone damage.

Thermal Burns

Thermal burns in chameleons usually occur when they are always near their basking light, or if the basking level is just too hot for them. Take note though that the skin doesn't actually have to touch the light for it to get burned. According to experts, chameleons' skin layer is very deep or far that's why they don't really know that their skins are getting burned. Always make sure that your basking light has the proper temperature to prevent thermal burns.

The usual signs of thermal burns are blisters, patches and redness but eventually it turns into black. The burned skin could also be peeled off. Usually there's a yellow discharge under the burned skin. The common spots for thermal burns are spine, casqued, and knees.

The great news is that thermal burns heal easily as long as there is proper care and chameleon husbandry.

If you discover that your chameleon has been suffering from burns, bring him to a vet immediately because bacterial infections or fungus can also happen if it is not immediately treated.

Sinus

If your chameleon's nose has bumps he may be suffering from a sinus infection. Sinus is usually caused by pus formation and swelling that can usually be seen near the nostrils. It can also be a cause or a sign of a respiratory infection. Pus formations are usually thick in reptiles, unlike in mammals where it is sort of a liquid form, so even if antibiotics are given to cure the primary infection it doesn't get rid of the pus that usually causes the swelling. Sinuses if not prevented can block the air pathway in the nostrils which can cause them to have difficulty in breathing. Once this happens, you vet may need to perform a minor surgery to open the nostril area in order to remove the pus.

Stomatitis

Stomatitis, also referred to as Mouth Rot is a systemic infection. You will see a yellowish pus or discharge in your chameleon's mouth if he has a stomatitis. Other signs of mouth rot that you need to watch out for include blackening of teeth, and swelling of the lips or its jaws.

If it is not treated, the bacterial infection can progress and affect your chameleon's jawbone as well as parts of its cranium which usually weakens the bones causing the teeth to become loose. It can also be potentially fatal. This illness needs vet treatment as soon as possible so that proper antibiotics and medication can be given, and so that the infected jaw can be cleaned.

Swollen Eyes

Swollen eyes are indicators of a blocked nasolacrimal duct. Once nasolacrimal duct is blocked it needs to be flushed. Antibiotics are usually given for this kind of infection. If the pus builds up under the eye socket your chameleon will need to undergo through surgery so that the vet can remove the pus and stop infections.

Don't be bothered when your chameleon bulge their eyes because it is how they clean or attempt to remove the dirt/foreign material inside their eyes, just watched out for bulgy eyes.

Foot Sores/ Pododermatitis

You might want to check if your chameleon is comfortable inside its cage or enclosure, especially the floor area. If the floor of your chameleon's enclosure is made out of chicken wire or any rough materials your chameleon can get abrasions from crawling on it. A skin infection in a chameleon's feet is called Pododermatitis; if the cage or its branches stays too moist this infection may form. Be sure to keep the environment dry so that it wouldn't cause further abrasion or major lesions. If you see the feet sores are discharging a liquid material, bring him to a reptile vet. If it is not immediately treated it can lead to a joint or it can also affect the bones, and it can cause serious injuries.

Gout / Swelling Joint

If you've seen the joints of your chameleon swelling, it's an indicator that he has developed gout. Gout is a very common illness among reptiles. Its main cause is excessive uric acid that is found in bloodstream. If there is too much uric acid, it usually develops into a salt crystal which then builds up in your chameleons joint.

There are two kinds of gout:

- Primary Gout – usually it is caused by too much dietary protein
- Secondary Gout – it is caused by dehydration or renal dysfunction among chameleons. It is the most common type of gout among these creatures.

Unfortunately, this condition cannot be treated; medications can only alleviate the pain but not necessarily stop it. You can however prevent it through proper husbandry, it is always the best defense against diseases; if the environment or the enclosure is always clean it can ultimately help your chameleon to have a healthy body.

The swelling of its joints is the result of the infected area inside the limb. A fluid sample may need to be given for laboratory analysis, and antibiotics should be taken. Your vet may also suggest cleaning or removing the affected joint to prevent it from spreading from other limb parts.

Diarrhea

Diarrhea just like in any animals or even humans is an intestinal disorder usually caused by intestinal parasites. The abnormal fecal frequency or the fluidity of the feces is the usual effect of diarrhea.

If your chameleon is suffering from diarrhea, he may have parasites in the intestine, bacterial overgrowth, or even inappropriate temperature which causes poor digestion, and leads to a different digestive cycle. A fecal sample is needed for an analysis by your reptile veterinarian.

Intestinal Parasites

Intestinal parasites are composed of microscopic worms and protozoa that basically lives inside you chameleon's intestine. These kinds of parasites are very common among captive bred chameleons.

Intestinal parasites are usually acquired from ingesting an infected or contaminated feeder as well as infected feces from other animals.

The usual signs of intestinal parasites are smelly feces, lethargy, weight loss and lack of appetite as well as vomiting.

These parasites are microscopic and therefore can't be seen by the naked eye, that's why you need to bring in a fresh fecal sample for laboratory analysis. Usually deworming medications are prescribed but it's not a one – size – fit – all, it still depends on the kind of parasite living inside your chameleon. A fecal sample is taken to find eggs of the parasites, however sometimes worms are don't shed eggs so a negative fecal test doesn't necessarily mean that your pet is free from parasites. Several fecal tests or samples should be submitted.

Chapter Nine: Frequently Ask Questions about Chameleons

Since chameleons are the kind of creatures that is not yet widely popular as a pet, or some may even call it an unconventional pet there are still lots of things you as the potential owner need to know. Unlike other pets you can't just go out and ask someone about how to care for a chameleon or what to do during an unexpected situation. Your best bet is find information on Google, join an online forum or ask someone in a social media community for chameleon enthusiasts. Check out some of the most frequently asks questions in this chapter so that you can use it for future reference.

- **Can I tame my chameleon? Can they trust me?**

Chameleon is general like any other pets have its own unique personality, unfortunately you can never tame or train your pet chameleon to be friendly (although if they get used to you they won't mind your human touch). Baby chameleons get stressed out if they are often handled. The best way to your chameleon's heart is probably through his stomach. Constant and consistent hand feeding might make you their trusted companion, but that's how far they can go. You really can't establish a connection with them like any other house pets.

- **Does my chameleon actually like me?**

Unfortunately almost all reptiles lack emotional capacity, you will never get a chance to bond with them and make them remember that "bonding time" you have, unlike cats or dogs. They don't even get emotionally attached to their own kind even if they are actually living in the same enclosure! The only positive experience that will stick with them is hand feeding, that's the only way you can get them to "like you."

- **Why won't my chameleon change color to match my shirt?**

Chameleons can't really change their color unless they are feeling threatened. They only change colors depending on their mood. So if they feel like they are in danger they use that ability as a defense mechanism.

A certain chameleon species or breeds have a set palette of colors that they use. For instance a terrified or stressed out chameleon will display dark colors such as black or dark blue; brighter colors are often a signal that they are in neutral mode like courtship or when they're resting. They can blend in and adjust to the color of their surrounding but not exactly match with the environment.

- **Can chameleons hear?**

Chameleons do not have any external ear structure, but they have an internal hearing capability somewhat similar to a snake. They hear things or become aware of their surroundings through vibration. They don't exactly hear things like humans do but they know if a music is loud or not through the degree of vibrations.

- **Does it hurt if a chameleon bites you?**

YES! These creatures even if they are small can hurt you, and if you get bitten by their small sharp teeth you can definitely bleed. Even if they don't really pierce you their pinch can be very painful. Some adult chameleons have a reputation for biting if they are angry or annoyed. If you get bitten just thoroughly wash the bite well.

- **What do you do about your chameleons if you need to go out of town?**

It's recommended that you retain the same schedule or routine. For example, you can get a cheap timer for your lights. If you will be gone for a day, they will survive without normal misting or food since the next schedule is still set for the following day.

If you'll be gone for more than a day or longer, then you'll definitely need somebody like a pet sitter who is not afraid of reptiles or bugs! He/she should be instructed on how to properly mist, feed and use the dripper. Make sure to automate your setup before going out of town.

- **Do I need to help my chameleon shed its skin?**

It's not recommended that you help your chameleon remove the shedding skin. The skin of a chameleon can be painful if peeled off or it can also damage the new skin underneath. The old skin will come off in due time, you can help them by increasing humidity levels so that the old skin can peel off easily and may expedite the shedding process.

- **Why is my chameleon's tongue not shooting out all the way/ missing the bugs/ not sticky?**

The chameleon's tongue has a very complex structure; it has delicate muscles that work in unison so there can be lots of different causes when it comes to tongue dysfunction. These dysfunctions may indicate a calcium imbalance or vitamin deficiency. Infections in the mouth or tongue will definitely affect the ability to shoot for its food correctly. If ever the tongue is left hanging out make sure to keep it moist and bring your chameleon to your vet immediately. If the tongue dries out or got bitten it may need to be amputated. Shooting problems can also be associated with eye problems as it will affect its aim.

- **I think my chameleon is suffering or dying. What is the best way to end their misery?**

If you think that your pet chameleon is dying, you should bring it to your vet for a human euthanasia so that it will minimize the pain and ease their suffering. Do not ever put a reptile in the refrigerator, contrary to popular belief, euthanizing a reptile by letting it freezing it inside the freezer will only make the animal not move but it doesn't necessarily numb the pain, in fact it makes it a slow death for them. This act is considered inhumane and illegal by the American Veterinary Medical Association.

- **Will Reptaid and herbal medications cure my sick chameleon?**

Herbal supplements such as ReptaBoost, Reptaid, and Critter Cure are not antibiotics. These herbal medicines are not approved by the Food and Drugs Administration (FDA), and the mere fact that there aren't any scientific or laboratory test supporting the claims that these supplements can cure an ill chameleon. Although these supplements are not directly harmful, it can still cause some side effects. If your chameleon has a respiratory or mouth infections, better buy an antibiotic prescribed by your veterinarian, and also follow the appropriate dosage.

- **I know which drug is used to commonly treat my chameleon's problem; can someone just give me the dose?**

Giving the proper dosage is not that simple, it highly depends on the type of medication, the type of illness or infection, the size, weight or age of the animal, the physical stat of your chameleon and its breed as well. There is no one – size – fits – all dosage, it will vary from one chameleon to another that is why you shouldn't apply any medication without a vet's instruction or prescription. If you use a medication or overdosed its amount it can definitely cause pathogen resistance or toxicity to your pet.

- **What kind of dewormer should I use for my chameleon?**

The dewormer should be recommended by your vet because it highly depends on the kind of parasites that is living inside your chameleon. Do not deworm your chameleon without first testing your chameleon's fecal sample. Just like any medication, dewormers are not supposed to be effective against all types of intestinal parasites, don't try to give something without consulting your vet first because you might administer the wrong type of medicine or an incorrect dosage. This could lead to resistance where the parasite evolves to be able survive the dewormer drug if not given appropriately, which can severely affect future treatment efforts.

Chameleons that have lots of intestinal parasite may also be dangerous even if the medication or dosage is appropriate because it can block the chameleon's intestine or could have an anaphylactic reaction to the dead parasites.

- **How can I give water to my chameleon that's not drinking?**

Don't force your chameleon to drink because it can choke them or cause pneumonia. Never open its mouth or squirt water directly on their mouth when they are hissing. Just increase the misting, try showering methods or improve your dripper set up. You can however force it to drink by feeding or offering a bug and slowly squirt a fair amount of water while it is still chewing the bug, once it stops to chew don't squirt water in its mouth anymore.

- **Can my female chameleon produce eggs even though there's no male?**

Yes, similar to chickens, chameleons can produce infertile egg (even without a male) around 5 – 6 months of age. Some chameleons may not be capable of doing that but most of them do. Just make sure to monitor your female's weight because an overweight female chameleon may tend to lay large egg clusters, and it can also cause complications during laying period.

- **When should I breed my chameleon?**

You should never breed your female chameleon until they are more than a year old. If you breed them at an early age while they are still growing at a high rate it can take calcium nutrients necessary for its bone and tissue growth because it will be needed to producing eggs.

- **I think my chameleon has eggs, what do I need to do to get her lay them?**

You may need to purchase or create a laying bin that is appropriate to your chameleon's size; this laying bin will encourage your female chameleon to lay her eggs. You can refer to several videos on YouTube if you want to know how to properly set up a laying bin for pregnant female chameleons. If she still can't lay eggs, she'll have a high risk of becoming egg – bound which is also a potentially life threatening condition. If she appears too weak during labor, better call your vet as soon as possible so that she can be given medications that will enable her to lay egg on her own, otherwise your vet may need to perform a c – section or else it could cause death your pet.

- **I was told that unless I mated my female that she would become egg-bound and die?**

This is not true simply because the chameleon's ability to lay eggs has nothing to do with the eggs being fertilized or not. There is no basis for this myth; as mentioned earlier, if you mate your female chameleon at a very young age it may cause significant health problems in the future.

- **How can I tell if my female is gravid or ready to breed?**

Your female chameleon's color patterns or shade will change indicating that she is ready or mature enough for breeding. Their color patterns indicate if they are gravid or receptive to breeding.

- **How can I tell if eggs are fertile?**

You can't tell if the eggs are fertilized just by merely observing it after being laid. You have to first incubate them (see breeding chapter), and it will usually take about 1 – 2 months before the eggs become fertile. During incubation, you can use a candle light to see if any blood vessels are present, that is a usual indicator that an embryo is growing. Still the ultimate test is if they are hatched or not.

Pygmy Leaf Chameleon Care Sheet

Congratulate yourself! You are now on your way to becoming a very well-informed and pro-active Pygmy Leaf Chameleon owner! Finishing this book is a huge milestone for you and your future or present pet chameleon, but before this ultimate guide comes to a conclusion, keep in mind the most important things you have acquired through reading this book. In the previous chapters, we have discussed the characteristics of a pygmy leaf, what it needs, the different tools you will need, the costs of keeping a pet chameleon, how to keep it healthy, and proper breeding practice. It may be a lot of information to take in, so we have compiled a care sheet to summarize the information you can find in this book.

Basic Information

- **Pedigree**: evolved from an iguana and lizard species
- **Breed Size:** relatively small and has a relatively elongated body structure similar to an iguana or a lizard.
- **Length:** adult length: 8 – 9 cm or 3 – 3.5 inches; smallest possible size: 2.5 cm or 1 inch
- **Weight:** very light
- **Coat Length**: coat is always changing depending on its environment; has a camouflage effect
- **Coat Texture**: quite rough, scaly
- **Color**: It has various shades of green, brown, yellow, grey and tone red.
- **Patterns/Markings:** It has various patterns resembling its natural habitat; spots
- **Feet Type:** similar to a lizard; small and webbed
- **Temperament**: docile, gentle, friendly, sensitive, delicate
- **Strangers**: may be threatened around strangers; may tend to vibrate or buzz
- **Other Pets**: can get along with other chameleon breed with no more than one male in an enclosure. Not advisable to introduce to other house pets.
- **Training**: cannot be trained, but behavior can be predicted

- **Exercise Needs**: doesn't need exercise; recommended as an observation pet only
- **Health Conditions**: generally healthy but predisposed to common illnesses such as lethargy, Metabolic Bone Disease, skin problems, burns head and neck issues, and other body syndromes
- **Lifespan**: average 1 to 3 years

Habitat Requirements

- **Recommended Equipment:** Cage (wooden or glass), terrarium or enclosure, dripper, substrate, live and artificial plants, UVB/ UVA light, heat bulb, misting equipment/ water spray, branches and vines
- **Recommended Day/Light Cycle:** 12-12 hours
- **Recommended Temperature:** 15 – 25 degrees Celsius or 60 – 78 degrees Fahrenheit
- **Recommended Humidity Levels:** 60 – 80% humidity
- **Cleaning Frequency:** clean at least once a day, regular spot cleaning.

Nutritional Needs

- **Primary Diet:** cricket, baby silkworms, baby hornworms
- **Feeding Frequency:**

  Neonates (0 to 3 months): feed them as many fruit flies or pinhead crickets as they can eat several times a day.

  Juveniles: (3 - 6 months): feed them around 6 - 10 small crickets daily.

  Adults: feed them 4 - 6 small crickets every other day

- **Water:** Fresh water through misting/dripping.
- **Primary gut – loading ingredients:** Turnip Greens, Collard Greens, Papaya, Escarole Lettuce, Watercress, Alfalfa, Mustard greens, Dandelion leaves
- **Secondary gut – loading ingredients:** Sweet Potato, Carrots, Butternut, Mango, Orange, Kale, Apples, Squash, Beet Greens, Bok Choy, Blackberries, Green beans
- **Dry gut – loading ingredients:** Organic and non – salted Sunflower seeds, bee pollen, dried seaweed, spirulina, flax seed, organic and non – salted almonds
- **Toxic gut – loading ingredients:** Cabbage, potatoes, Iceberg Lettuce, Romain Lettuce, Spinach, Broccoli, Tomatoes, Grains, Corns, Oats, Beans, Meat, Eggs,

Cereals, Cat food/ Dog Food, Fish food, canned/ dead insects.

Breeding Information

- **Age of Sexual Maturity:** 1 year old
- **Number of eggs:** around 10 eggs or more
- **Incubation Period:** 45 – 90 days
- **Recommended Incubation Temperatures:** 18 – 25 degrees Celsius or 65 – 78F
- **Recommended Temperature Levels for Neonate:** 24 degrees Celsius or 76 degrees Fahrenheit

Index

D

E

F

G

S

T

Photo Credits

Page 1 Frank Vassen Photo by via Flickr.com,

<https://www.flickr.com/photos/42244964@N03/3899499361/
>

Page 15 Satoshi Tomiyama Photo by via Flickr.com,

<https://www.flickr.com/photos/nextlevelplus/4423205298/>

Page 26 Matt Zimmerman Photo by via Flickr.com,

<https://www.flickr.com/photos/16725630@N00/953293753/>

Page 39 Photo by Ken Clifton via Flickr.com,

<https://www.flickr.com/photos/by-ken/4158872536/>

Page 53 Matt Zimmerman Photo by via Flickr.com,

<https://www.flickr.com/photos/16725630@N00/954418848/>

Page 63 Photo by Gerard Van der Leun via Flickr.com,

<https://www.flickr.com/photos/1000photosofnewyorkcity/4
481783591/>

Page 72 Photo by Satoshi Tomiyama via Flickr.com,

<https://www.flickr.com/photos/nextlevelplus/4423204946/>

Page 76 Photo by groucho via Flickr.com,

<https://www.flickr.com/photos/groucho/3025889020/>

Page 81 Photo by Keultjes via Flickr.com,

<https://commons.wikimedia.org/wiki/File:Rieppeleon_kerst
enii.jpg>

Page 93 Photo by Bernard Dupont via Flickr.com,

<https://www.flickr.com/photos/berniedup/7629587464/>

Page 105 Photo by PeacockArmageddon via Flickr.com,

<https://www.flickr.com/photos/harby/8832040184/in/photol
ist>

References

"A Cute and Tiny Pygmy Chameleon" Featured Creature
<https://featuredcreature.com/cute-tiny-pygmy-chameleon/>

"Average Cost of Owning a Chameleon"
Chameleon Forums
<https://www.chameleonforums.com/blogs/average-cost-of-owning-a-chameleon.522/>

"Brookesia Minima" Wikipedia
<https://en.wikipedia.org/wiki/Brookesia_minima>

"Chameleons and the CITE Law" My Pet Chameleon
<http://mypetchameleon.com/buying-a-chameleon/chameleons-and-the-cites-law/>

"Chameleon Facts" Livescience.con
<http://www.livescience.com/51061-chameleon.html>

"Chameleon Health" Chameleon Forums
<https://www.chameleonforums.com/care/health/>

"Food and Nutrition" Chameleon Forums
<https://www.chameleonforums.com/care/food/>

"Frequently Ask Questions" Chameleon Forums
<https://www.chameleonforums.com/care/faq/>

"Husbandry of Montane Species of Chameleons"
LLL Reptile

<https://www.lllreptile.com/articles/220-husbandry-of-montane-species-of-chameleons/>

"Keeping Pygmy Chameleons" Arcadia - Reptile
<http://arcadia-reptile.com/keeping-pygmy-chameleons/>

"Keeping Pygmy Chameleons as Pets" Pets4Homes UK
<https://www.pets4homes.co.uk/pet-advice/keeping-pygmy-chameleons-as-pets.html>

"Purchasing a Chameleon" Chameleon Forums
<https://www.chameleonforums.com/care/purchasing/>

"Pygmy Care Sheet" Chameleon Forums
<https://www.chameleonforums.com/care/caresheets/pygmy />

"Pygmy Chameleon" Chameleon Forums
<https://www.chameleonforums.com/care/caresheets/pygmy
/>

"Pygmy Leaf Chameleon" Lizard Spirit Art
<https://lizardspritart.jimdo.com/brevicaudatus-pygmy-leaf-
chameleon-care/>

"What are the Pros and Cons of Chameleon as a Pet"
Wise Geek
<http://www.wisegeek.org/what-are-the-pros-and-cons-of-a-
chameleon-as-a-pet.htm>

"Your First Chameleon" Author: Bill Strand.
ChameleonBreeder.com

<http://www.chameleonbreeder.com/wp-
content/uploads/2016/07/Your-First-Chameleon-Web-
070316.pdf>

Feeding Baby
Cynthia Cherry
978-1941070000

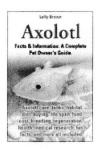

Axolotl
Lolly Brown
978-0989658430

Dysautonomia, POTS
Syndrome
Frederick Earlstein
978-0989658485

Degenerative Disc
Disease Explained
Frederick Earlstein
978-0989658485

Sinusitis, Hay Fever,
Allergic Rhinitis Explained
Frederick Earlstein
978-1941070024

Wicca
Riley Star
978-1941070130

Zombie Apocalypse
Rex Cutty
978-1941070154

Capybara
Lolly Brown
978-1941070062

Eels As Pets
Lolly Brown
978-1941070167

Scabies and Lice Explained
Frederick Earlstein
978-1941070017

Saltwater Fish As Pets
Lolly Brown
978-0989658461

Torticollis Explained
Frederick Earlstein
978-1941070055

Kennel Cough
Lolly Brown
978-0989658409

Physiotherapist, Physical Therapist
Christopher Wright
978-0989658492

Rats, Mice, and Dormice As Pets
Lolly Brown
978-1941070079

Wallaby and Wallaroo Care
Lolly Brown
978-1941070031

Bodybuilding Supplements
Explained
Jon Shelton
978-1941070239

Demonology
Riley Star
978-19401070314

Pigeon Racing
Lolly Brown
978-1941070307

Dwarf Hamster
Lolly Brown
978-1941070390

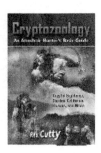

Cryptozoology
Rex Cutty
978-1941070406

Eye Strain
Frederick Earlstein
978-1941070369

Inez The Miniature Elephant
Asher Ray
978-1941070353

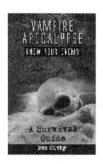

Vampire Apocalypse
Rex Cutty
978-1941070321

Printed in Great Britain
by Amazon

38848918R00076